Giggle Fit

Tricky Tongue-Twisters

Illustrated by
Steve Harpster

Joseph Rosenbloom

Sterling Publishing Co., Inc. New York

Library of Congress Cataloging-in-Publication Data Available

1   3   5   7   9   10   8   6   4   2

Published by Sterling Publishing Company, Inc.
387 Park Avenue South, New York, N.Y. 10016
© 2001 by Joseph Rosenbloom
Distributed in Canada by Sterling Publishing
$^{C}/o$ Canadian Manda Group, One Atlantic Avenue, Suite 105
Toronto, Ontario, Canada M6K 3E7
Distributed in Great Britain and Europe by Chris Lloyd at
Orca Book Services, Stanley House, Fleets Lane, Poole BH15 3AJ, England
Distributed in Australia by Capricorn Link (Australia) Pty. Ltd.
P.O. Box 704, Windsor, NSW 2756 Australia
Printed in China

Sterling ISBN 0-8069-8018-4

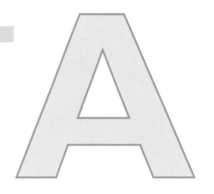

Aunt Edith's anteater.
Aunt Edith's anteater.
Aunt Edith's anteater.

Ava ate 80 eggs.
Ava ate 80 eggs.
Ava ate 80 eggs.

Ape cakes.
Ape cakes.
Ape cakes.

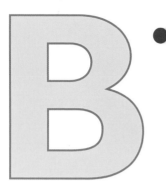

B

Build a big brick building.
Build a big brick building.
Build a big brick building

A box of biscuits.
A box of biscuits.
A box of biscuits.

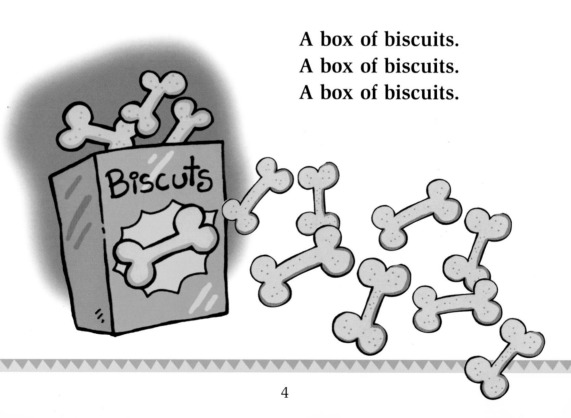

Rubber baby buggy bumpers.
Rubber baby buggy bumpers.
Rubber baby buggy bumpers.

How many times can you say this in ten seconds?
Brown, black, blue.

Bluebirds in blue birdbaths.
Bluebirds in blue birdbaths.
Bluebirds in blue birdbaths.

Bedbug's blood.
Bedbug's blood.
Bedbug's blood.

Betty Botter bought a bit of butter.
"But," said she, "this butter's bitter.
If I put in in my batter, it will make my batter bitter.
But a bit of better butter — that would make my
             batter better."
So Better Botter bought a bit of better butter
(Better than her bitter butter)
And made her bitter butter
A bit better.

Crisp crust crackles.
Crisp crust crackles.
Crisp crust crackles.

Cheap sausage stew.
Cheap sausage stew.
Cheap sausage stew

Clean clams.
Clean clams.
Clean clams.

The fish and chip shop.
The fish and chip shop.
The fish and chip shop.

Tricky crickets.
Tricky crickets.
Tricky crickets.

Crisp cracker crumbs.
Crisp cracker crumbs.
Crisp cracker crumbs.

Chip's ship sank.
Chip's ship sank.
Chip's ship sank.

Carl called Claude.
Carl called Claude.
Carl called Claude.

Kookie cookies.
Kookie cookies.
Kookie cookies.

How many times can you say this in ten seconds?
Jerry chewed two chewy cherries.

Chris's craft crashed.
Chris's craft crashed.
Chris's craft crashed.

Cheap sheep soup.
Cheap sheep soup.
Cheap sheep soup.

Don't you dare dawdle, Darryl!
Don't you dare dawdle, Darryl!
Don't you dare dawdle, Darryl!

A dozen dim ding-dongs.
A dozen dim ding-dongs.
A dozen dim ding-dongs.

Ducks don't dunk doughnuts.
Ducks don't dunk doughnuts.
Ducks don't dunk doughnuts.

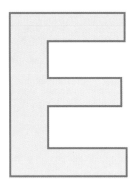

E

Eight eager eagles.
Eight eager eagles.
Eight eager eagles.

Edgar at 8 ate 8 eggs a day.
Edgar at 8 ate 8 eggs a day.
Edgar at 8 ate 8 eggs a day.

Elegant elephants.
Elegant elephants.
Elegant elephants.

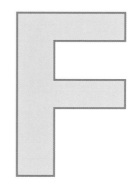

Fried fresh fish.
Fried fresh fish.
Fried fresh fish.

Fifteen filthy flying foxes.
Fifteen filthy flying foxes.
Fifteen filthy flying foxes.

Free kiwis.
Free kiwis.
Free kiwis.

Five fat French fleas.
Five fat French fleas.
Five fat French fleas.

Fresh figs.
Fresh figs.
Fresh figs.

Four flyers flip-flop.
Four flyers flip-flop.
Four flyers flip-flop.

How many times can you say this
in ten seconds?
Frisk Fisk first.

Free fruit flies.
Free fruit flies.
Free fruit flies.

Freckle-faced Freddy fidgets.
Freckle-faced Freddy fidgets.
Freckle-faced Freddy fidgets.

Frank flunked French.
Frank flunked French.
Frank flunked French.

Fleas fly from flies.
Fleas fly from flies.
Fleas fly from flies.

Frank's friend fainted.
Frank's friend fainted.
Frank's friend fainted.

Greek grapes.
Greek grapes.
Greek grapes.

Good blood, bad blood.
Good blood, bad blood.
Good blood, bad blood.

Goats and ghosts.
Goats and ghosts.
Goats and ghosts.

17

H

Hiccup teacup.
Hiccup teacup.
Hiccup teacup.

Has Hal's heel healed?
Has Hal's heel healed?
Has Hal's heel healed?

Hugh chooses huge shoes.
Hugh chooses huge shoes.
Hugh chooses huge shoes.

How many times can you say this in ten seconds?

Horse hairs are coarse hairs, of course.

Hurry, Harry!
Hurry, Harry!
Hurry, Harry!

A black spotted haddock.
A black spotted haddock.
A black spotted haddock.

Higgledy-Piggledy.
Higgledy-Piggledy.
Higgledy-Piggledy.

If a Hottentot taught
A Hottentot tot
To talk ere the tot could totter,
Ought the Hottentot tot
Be taught to say "ought"
Or what ought to be taught her?

I see Isa's icy eyes.
I see Isa's icy eyes.
I see Isa's icy eyes.

Ike ships ice chips.
Ike ships ice chips.
Ike ships ice chips.

A gentle judge judges justly.
A gentle judge judges justly.
A gentle judge judges justly.

Jim jogs in the gym. Jane jogs in the jungle.

June sheep
sleep soundly.

22

Come kick six sticks.
Come kick six sticks.
Come kick six sticks.

This disk sticks.
This disk sticks.
This disk sticks.

How many times can you say this
in ten seconds?
Kirk's starched shirts.

Kooky kite kits.
Kooky kite kits.
Kooky kite kits.

23

L

Red leather. Yellow leather.
Red leather. Yellow leather.
Red leather. Yellow leather.

Little Ida lied a lot.
Little Ida lied a lot.
Little Ida lied a lot.

Lily Little lit a little lamp.
Lily Little lit a little lamp.
Lily Little lit a little lamp.

Luke likes licorice.
Luke likes licorice.
Luke likes licorice.

Lizzie's dizzy lizard.
Lizzie's dizzy lizard.
Lizzie's dizzy lizard.

How many times can you say this in ten seconds?
Loose loops.

Mummies munch much mush.
Mummies munch much mush.
Mummies munch much mush.

Moses supposes his toeses are roses,
But Moses supposes erroneously.
For nobody's toeses are posies of roses
As Moses supposes his toeses to be.

How many times can you say this in ten seconds?
Michael's mouse
munched muffins.

How many times can you say this in ten seconds?

No one knows Wayne.

**There's no need to light a night light
On a light night like tonight,
For a night light's just a slight light,
On a light night like tonight.**

**Norse myths.
Norse myths.
Norse myths.**

**Nineteen nice knights.
Nineteen nice knights.
Nineteen nice knights.**

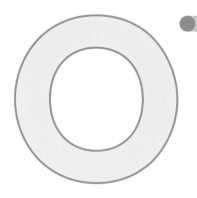

Old oily corks.
Old oily corks.
Old oily corks.

An oyster met an oyster,
And they were oysters two.
Two oysters met two oysters,
And they were oysters too.
Four oysters met a pint of milk,
And they were oyster stew.

Under the mother otter,
Uttered the other otter.

Plain bun, plum bun.
Plain bun, plum bun.
Plain bun, plum bun.

Peter Piper picked a peck of
    pickled peppers,
A peck of pickled peppers,
Peter Piper picked.
If Peter Piper picked a peck of
    pickled peppers,
Where's the peck of pickled
    peppers Peter Piper
    picked?

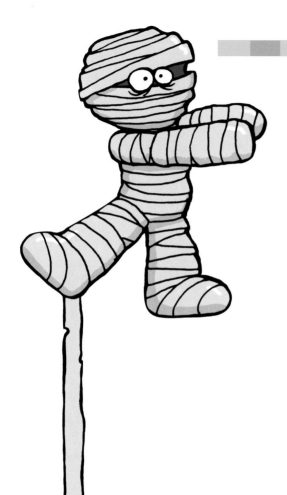

Peggy Babcock's mummy.
Peggy Babcock's mummy.
Peggy Babcock's mummy.

Painters, planters, pointers.
Painters, planters, pointers.
Painters, planters, pointers.

How many times can you say this in ten seconds?

Penny penned a pretty poem.

Picky pickpockets.
Picky pickpockets.
Picky pickpockets.

Preshrunk shirts.
Preshrunk shirts.
Preshrunk shirts.

Pooped purple pelicans.
Pooped purple pelicans.
Pooped purple pelicans.

*How many times can you say this
in ten seconds?*
Quick kiss.

Quincy! Quack quietly or quit quacking!
Quincy! Quack quietly or quit quacking!
Quincy! Quack quietly or quit quacking!

Rigid wicker rockers.
Rigid wicker rockers.
Rigid wicker rockers.

How many times can you say this in ten seconds?
A well-read redhead.

The rhino wore a white ribbon.
The rhino wore a white ribbon.
The rhino wore a white ribbon.

Really rich roaches wear wristwatches.

Raise Ruth's roof.
Raise Ruth's roof.
Raise Ruth's roof.

Red wrens' wings.
Red wrens' wings.
Red wrens' wings.

Robin robs wealthy widows.

Mrs. Smith's Fish Soup Shop.
Mrs. Smith's Fish Soup Shop.
Mrs. Smith's Fish Soup Shop.

The sun shines on shop signs.
The sun shines on shop signs.
The sun shines on shop signs.

Of all the smells I ever smelled,
I never smelled a smell
Like that smelt I smelled smelt.

Six slick seals.
Six slick seals.
Six slick seals.

How many times can you say this in ten seconds?

Spicy fish sauce.

"Sure, the ship's ship-shape, sir!"

Six sick shorn sheep.
Six sick shorn sheep.
Six sick shorn sheep.

Short swords.
Short swords.
Short swords.

*How many times can you say this
in ten seconds?*

Sloppy shortstops.

Sneak thieves seized the skis.
Sneak thieves seized the skis.
Sneak thieves seized the skis.

Stagecoach stops.
Stagecoach stops.
Stagecoach stops.

**She sells seashells by
the seashore.**

Mr. Spink thinks the Sphinx stinks.
Mr. Spink thinks the Sphinx stinks.
Mr. Spink thinks the Sphinx stinks.

A knapsack strap.
A knapsack strap.
A knapsack strap.

A skunk sat on a stump.
The skunk thunk the stump
      stunk,
But the stump thunk the
      skunk stunk.

Do thick tinkers think?
Do thick tinkers think?
Do thick tinkers think?

*How many times can you say this
in ten seconds?*
Thistle thorns stick.

A tutor who tooted a flute
Tried to tutor two tooters to toot.
Said the two to the tutor,
"Is it harder to toot
Or to tutor two tooters to toot?"

A tree toad loved a she-toad
That lived up in a tree.
She was a three-toed tree toad,
But a two-toed toad was he.

The two-toed toad tried to win
The she-toad's friendly nod,
For the two-toed toad loved the ground
On which the three-toed tree toad trod,

But no matter how the two-toad tree toad tried,
He could not please her whim.
In her three-toed bower, with her three-toed power,
The three-toed she-toad vetoed him.

Three free through trains.

Twelve trim twin-track tapes.
Twelve trim twin-track tapes.
Twelve trim twin-track tapes.

Tacky tractor trailer trucks.

Thick thistle sticks.

Ted sent Stan ten tents.
Ted sent Stan ten tents.
Ted sent Stan ten tents.

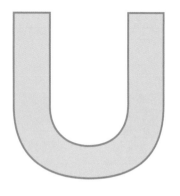

The U.S. twin-screw cruiser.
The U.S. twin-screw cruiser.
The U.S. twin-screw cruiser.

How many times can you say this in ten seconds?
Unique New York.

Uncle Upton's undies.
Uncle Upton's undies.
Uncle Upton's undies.

Vandals waxed Valerie's white van.
Vandals waxed Valerie's white van.
Vandals waxed Valerie's white van.

Valuable valley villas.
Valuable valley villas.
Valuable valley villas.

How many times can you say this in ten seconds?
Which veteran ventriloquist whistled?

Real wristwatch straps.

Whether the weather be fine
Or whether the weather be not;
Whether the weather be cold,
Or whether the weather be hot;
We'll weather the weather
Whatever the weather,
Whether we like it or not.

How many times can you say this in ten seconds?

An itchy rich witch.

44

How much wood would a
	woodchuck chuck
If a woodchuck could
	chuck wood?
He would chuck the wood
	as much as he could
If a woodchuck could
	chuck wood.

White rings, round rings.
White rings, round rings.
White rings, round rings.

Wire-rimmed wheels.
Wire-rimmed wheels.
Wire-rimmed wheels.

X

Ex-disk jockey.
Ex-disk jockey.
Ex-disk jockey.

Xmas wrecks perplex and vex.
Xmas wrecks perplex and vex.
Xmas wrecks perplex and vex.

Yellow leather, red feather.

Yanking yellow yo-yos.
Yanking yellow yo-yos.
Yanking yellow yo-yos.

Local yokel jokes.

This is a zither.
Is this a zither?

INDEX